MW00628051

FROM PANDEMIC TO PROMISE

WRITTEN BY:
DR. VALERIE DANIELS-CARTER

Copyright ©2020 by Dr. Valerie Daniels-Carter
All rights reserved.

Scripture quotations noted KJV are from the King James Version of the Bible.

While every effort has been made to trace copyright holders, the publisher will promptly rectify any errors or omissions upon notification.

Published by:
Chronicle Publishing
Milwaukee, WI

Cover design by: Pastor Gerald Hill and DeMonica Flagg

Printed In The United States Of America
ISBN 978-1-63649-315-2

Books also by Dr. Valerie Daniels-Carter

- His Business Is Your Business, It's Where Destiny Takes You.
- Anointed Offering or Tainted Sacrifice

Dedication

Coronavirus has had a personal effect on my life this year. I have experienced the loss of dear friends and loving relatives. This Pandemic has indeed pierced the very fibers of my heart, more than what I could ever express in words.

I would like to dedicate this book to my uncle Chancellor Alton E. Townsel more affectionately known as "Uncle Gene" or "Chubby". A corrective grammar genius, he would have been waiting patiently, with pen in hand, to be my first reader and editor of this work. For countless years he edited and reviewed the literary work of various authors. As shared by Bishop Sedgwick Daniels in Alton's Chronology of Life, "His pursuit to overcome cultural and societal barriers afforded him stellar accomplishments and recognition as a public-school teacher and administrator. He demonstrated an exceptional ability to excel in his educational pursuits, and defined an unparalleled academic protocol, which was celebrated by his superiors, contemporaries, and subordinates. Alton's notable accomplishments afforded him numerous ascendancies, commendations, and promotions in every area of his concentration as an academician.

Moreover, as a revered administrator, Brother Townsel influenced positive and progressive collaborations within his community that enhanced and empowered families. He exemplified a regal demeanor, encircled a profound adroitness, and epitomized a prognostic expectation. His meritorious acclaims were achieved through the unwavering support of his family, who promoted and advanced every aspect of his development and accomplishments. His phenomenal and adulate commitment serves as an archetype to future generations and silhouettes a profound example of a gentlemen committed to academic rigor and educational excellence."

Chancellor Townsel, my "Uncle Gene", will forever be missed; but his legacy, influence, and the love he shared with incalculable thousands, will continue to live on for ages to come. He planted unselfishly in the lives of others and now he has been bequeathed eternal life. If heaven needs any literally work edited for precise clarity, it now has a champion in language rules who has been elevated to the halls of Glory.

FROM PANDEMIC TO PROMISE

Contents

FROM PANDEMIC TO PROMISE

The Forward

The world descended into colossal tumult and widespread chaos at the beginning of the first quarter of 2020 due to an insidious virus called corona virus disease (Covid-19). Disruptions of this magnitude could only emanate from a sordid and apocalyptic imagination just one year ago. Since the virus maneuvered its way onto the shores of the United States, swaths of businesses have literally died a thousand deaths at an alarmingly disturbing rate. Airlines have altered their flying routes to strikingly unprecedented lows, the financial markets have experienced treacherous fluctuations and volatility, a veritable harvest of jobs has dissolved into oblivion and food supplies have been fleeced from grocery store shelves at Armageddon like levels, due to government efforts to contain the virus. Governments have mandated dystopian curfews, which assigned entire families into what feels like burrowing away in Siberian concentration camps. Social gatherings are deemed a distant luxury and erstwhile large-scale events have dwindled into unrecognizable conclaves pierced by a litany of restrictions. Innumerable human bodies of sundry configurations, hues and ages have been mercilessly infected, and an unacceptably elevated number of human bodies have been ravished unto death. An unending web of local, state, and national injunctions have severely remodeled the freedom of its wearied and debilitated citizenry. With morally vacuous leadership and terrifying levels of infantile political partisanship, any prospects of relief appear haplessly elusive.

Why This Pandemic, Why Now? Back in April of this year, Jewish people celebrated Passover and Christians recognized the death of Jesus on the Cross on Good Friday as people throughout the world continued to suffer from coronavirus. Strangely, the anatomical meaning of the word corona is crown. In astrophysics, the word corona relates to rarefied gas enveloping the sun. One could creatively connote the corona virus as a "crown on the sun," almost an irreverent attack and mocking of the "Crown on the Son," (Jesus our Savior). There is a cosmic, existential war in the spirit realm and God is maneuvering Creation towards a cleansing and an awakening, or a virtual "turning opportunity." We all face an eternal choice to pivot from the cloak of darkness towards the liberating embrace of light and spiritual renewal.

Notwithstanding, a great chasm and void have been created relative to locating and establishing any substantive solutions. Over recent months, there have been myriad of feeble suggestions, spurious conspiracies, and squalid pontifications. Even those in the hallowed halls of "episteme" the self- appointed purveyors of science and virology appear to be rather vexed and flummoxed regarding the exact nature and trajectory of the coronavirus. But there is a Word from the Lord! The esteemed founder of Methodism, John Wesley, said "Without God, man cannot and without man, God will not." This often-mysterious synergy and interplay with our Creator must be hearkened unto with voracious intent and focus during this perilous epoch. We must approach His throne with all due humility and obedience. For we cannot find answers and God will not act if we choose to ignore seeking and praying for His divine intervention. An in-depth study of the Bible confirms that in each and every case, God has never left His people without hope or solutions. Therefore, I would like to evoke some helpful insights and thoughts from a biblical perspective.

It is highly apropos for humanity to audaciously ruminate on the query, "What can we learn from the coronavirus experience that will enable us to lead fuller and more meaningful lives? How can we find a deeper spiritual meaning from this experience?"

As I personally contemplate on these questions, a flow of considerations shower the expanse of logical deduction:

- We are realizing just how superficial our materialistic desires have become.
- We are reconnecting with our families in new and more meaningful ways.
- We are appreciating the importance of community and finding new ways to create community.
- We are recognizing what is truly important in life and the role that love plays in our lives.
- We are recommitting to make a difference in the world, using our gifts to help other people.
- We are caring for each other even as we are separated and learning to be connected while apart.
- We are learning again just how precious our health is to us.

- We are asking ourselves whether all of our "busyness" leads to a more fulfilled life.
- We are exploring our spiritual lives again, trusting in our belief in the Higher Power.
- We believe that we will emerge from this experience wiser, more caring, and more intentional in living our lives with meaning.

As you read The Promise chapter, contained therein are facts or ideas termed "Nuggets of Wisdom" for your consideration.

The Pandemic

I asked myself, what is a Pandemic? Let me first make a distinction between the terms pandemic and epidemic. Typically, an epidemic is an illness or disease that affects a vast number of people within a specific community, population or region. Epidemiologically, a pandemic is an epidemic that spreads to involve other countries or continents with no regard to one's status, creed, or color. One such example is the Bubonic Plague (Black Death) that killed massive numbers of people in the mid - 1300's. It most often spreads across regions, countries, continents and even worldwide. Both epidemics and pandemics have a common root word – "demic". As defined in the *Free Dictionary by Farlex*, "demic" means "a characteristic of or pertaining to a people or population." So, in essence, they both deal with something that has a global effect on scores of people.

Let us consider for a moment the term plague, which is derived from several words in the original biblical languages. From a biblical perspective,

Easton's Bible Dictionary defines a Plague as "a stroke of affliction or disease sent as a divine chastisement."

The unimagined tragic toll that epidemics, pandemics or plagues if you will, take on the lives of people of sundry hues; disparate life experiences and generations traverse socioeconomic strata without respect to one's station in life. A beautiful, astute, well accomplished young lady as well as a handsome, distinguished, well positioned gentleman can be on top of the world one day, though when subject to the ravishing of a pandemic they become helpless, hapless and dependent on others and a Higher Being for survival.

Pandemics can attack a newborn baby with equal ferocity as it does an athletically inclined young adult. When not properly addressed, Pandemics can destroy the very fiber of one's life. You cannot legislate it away, wish it away, or give it away. Once it attaches to you, it takes God to completely heal you. Medicines and vaccines can aid in controlling some of its symptoms and spread, but quite often there remains an ominous scar from its presence, be it emotional or physical.

The bible is replete with references to plaques spanning from the Book of Genesis through Revelation.

Genesis 12:17 - And the LORD plagued Pharaoh and his house with great plagues because of Sarai Abram's wife.

Exodus 9:14 - For I will at this time send all my plagues upon thine heart, and upon thy servants, and upon thy people; that thou mayest know that there is none like me in all the earth.

Leviticus 26:21 - And if ye walk contrary unto me and will not hearken unto me; I will bring seven times more plagues upon you according to your sins.

Deuteronomy 28:59 - Then the LORD will make thy plagues wonderful, and the plagues of thy seed, even great plagues, and of long continuance, and sore sicknesses, and of long continuance.

Deuteronomy 29:22 - So that the generation to come of your children that shall rise up after you, and the stranger that shall come from a far land, shall say, when they see the plagues of that land, and the sicknesses which the LORD hath laid upon it.

1 Samuel 4:8 - Woe unto us! who shall deliver us out of the hand of these mighty Gods? these are the Gods that smote the Egyptians with all the plagues in the wilderness.

We should always have a sense of appreciation for the landmarks and mishaps of the past. Wisdom teaches us this lesson over and over. One of the most significant reasons historical pandemics resonate with people is because they were unique in nature and devastating to the masses.

However, behind each occurrence, we see an extraordinary miracle or way of escape. The bible is replete with examples of what happens when human beings experience setbacks and how an extraordinary God bring deliverance during these circumstances. As we review the plaques of yesteryear, I ask the question: Are we prepared during this extraordinary time, to take extraordinary leaps of faith and pursue purpose?

Jeremiah 19:8 - And I will make this city desolate, and a hissing; every one that passeth thereby shall be astonished and hiss because of all the plagues thereof.

Jeremiah 49:17 - Also Edom shall be a desolation: everyone that goeth by it shall be astonished and shall hiss at all the plagues thereof.

Jeremiah 50:13 - Because of the wrath of the LORD it shall not be inhabited, but it shall be wholly desolate: everyone that goeth by Babylon shall be astonished, and hiss at all her plagues.

Hosea 13:14 - I will ransom them from the power of the grave; I will redeem them from death: O death, I will be thy plagues; O grave, I will be thy destruction: repentance shall be hid from mine eyes.

Mark 3:10 - For he had healed many; insomuch that they pressed upon him for to touch him, as many as had plagues.

Luke 7:21 - And in that same hour he cured many of their infirmities and plagues, and of evil spirits; and unto many that were blind he gave sight.

The fact that we see plaques referenced in the book of Revelation indicates to me that we have not seen all there is to come.

Revelation 9:20 - And the rest of the men which were not killed by these plagues yet repented not of the works of their hands, that they should not worship devils, and idols of gold, and silver, and brass, and stone, and of wood: which neither can see, nor hear, nor walk:

Revelation 11:6 - These have power to shut heaven that it rain not in the days of their prophecy: and have power over waters to turn them to blood, and to smite the earth with all plagues, as often as they will.

Revelation 15:1 - And I saw another sign in heaven, great and marvelous, seven angels having the seven last plagues; for in them is filled up the wrath of God.

Revelation 15:6 - And the seven angels came out of the temple, having the seven plagues, clothed in pure and white linen, and having their breasts girded with golden girdles.

Revelation 15:8 - And the temple was filled with smoke from the glory of God, and from his power; and no man was able to enter into the temple, till the seven plagues of the seven angels were fulfilled.

Revelation 16:9 - And men were scorched with great heat, and blasphemed the name of God, which hath power over these plagues: and they repented not to give him glory.

Revelation 18:4 - And I heard another voice from heaven, saying, Come out of her, my people, that ye be not partakers of her sins, and that ye receive not of her plagues.

Revelation 18:8 - Therefore shall her plagues come in one day, death, and mourning, and famine; and she shall be utterly burned with fire: for strong is the Lord God who judgeth her.

Revelation 21:9 - And there came unto me one of the seven angels which had the seven vials full of the seven last plagues, and talked with me, saying, Come hither, I will shew thee the bride, the Lamb's wife.

Revelation 22:18 - For I testify unto every man that heareth the words of the prophecy of this book, If any man shall add unto these things, God shall add unto him the plagues that are written in this book.

- **NUGGET OF WISDOM**: **Don't Be Weary Or Fearful Because Purpose and Promise Have Always Been Spiritual Protectants from Pain and Suffering.**

The Bible records ten plagues in the book of Exodus. The ten plagues include agricultural afflictions such as locusts; diseases such as boils; supernatural or astronomical plagues such as storms or fire or darkness; and, finally, the tenth plague — the killing of all firstborn Egyptian sons.

The Ten Plagues are as follows:

- Water turned to blood (Exodus 7:14-25).
- Frogs cover the land (Exodus 8:1-15).
- The dust turns into gnats or lice (Exodus 8:16-19).
- Swarms of flies cover the land (Exodus 8:20-32).
- Death of all Egyptian livestock (Exodus 9:1-7).

- Boils break out on the people of Egypt (Exodus 9:8-12).
- Hailstorms kill unsheltered humans, animals, and vegetation (Exodus 9:13-35).
- Locusts cover the land and consume all remaining vegetation (Exodus 10:1-20).
- Darkness covers Egypt for three days (Exodus 10:21-29).
- The firstborn children of all Egyptian people and cattle die (Exodus 11:1-10, 12:29-32).

The Jews were eventually able to escape the plagues by smearing lamb blood over their doors. The ten sequential disasters God inflicted on Egypt generally increased in intensity as they progressed. As a result of the plagues, the Pharaoh of Egypt ultimately released the Israelites. But after releasing the Israelites, Pharaoh was determined to resume his pursuit.

The question comes to mind, **"Why and How Does A loving God Allow Such To Be"?** We will address this matter in the chapter called "The Promise." But let us look at this in a historical context.

According to *History.com*, the pandemic which occurred in Athens in 430 B.C. is the earliest recorded pandemic. This, of course, is a reference from a non-biblical source. This particular pandemic happened during the Peloponnesian War. After the disease passed through Libya, Ethiopia, and Egypt, it crossed the Athenian walls as the Spartans laid siege. As many as two-thirds of the population died. The symptoms included fever, thirst, a bloody throat and tongue, red skin, and lesions. The disease, suspected to have been typhoid fever, weakened the Athenians significantly and was a compelling factor in their defeat by the Spartans.

The chronological order is listed by *History.com* as follows:

165 A.D.: Antonine Plague

The Antonine Plague was possibly an early appearance of smallpox that began with the Huns. The Huns then infected the Germans, who passed it to the Romans and then returning troops spread it throughout the Roman Empire. Symptoms included fever, sore throat, and diarrhea; if the patient lived long enough, he or she developed pus-filled sores. This plague continued until about 180 A.D., claiming Emperor Marcus Aurelius as one of its victims.

250 A.D.: Cyprian Plague

Named after the first known victim, the Christian Bishop of Carthage, the Cyprian Plague entailed diarrhea, vomiting, throat ulcers, fever and gangrenous hands and feet.

City dwellers fled to the country to escape infection but instead spread the disease further. Possibly starting in Ethiopia, it passed through Northern Africa, into Rome, then onto Egypt and northward.

There were recurring outbreaks over the next three centuries. In 444 A.D., it hit Britain and obstructed defense efforts against the Picts and the Scots, causing the British to seek help from the Saxons, who would soon control the island.

541 A.D.: Justinian Plague

First appearing in Egypt, the Justinian Plague spread through Palestine and the Byzantine Empire, and then throughout the Mediterranean.

The plague changed the course of the empire, squelching Emperor Justinian's plans to bring the Roman Empire back together and causing massive economic struggle. It is also credited with creating an apocalyptic atmosphere that spurred the rapid spread of Christianity.

Recurrences over the next two centuries eventually killed about 50 million people, 26 percent of the world population. It is believed to be the first significant appearance of the Bubonic Plague, which featured enlarged lymphatic glands and was carried by rats and spread by fleas.

11th Century: Leprosy

Though it had been around for ages, leprosy grew into a pandemic in Europe in the Middle Ages, resulting in the building of numerous leprosy-focused hospitals to accommodate the vast number of victims.

A slow-developing bacterial disease that causes sores and deformities, leprosy was believed to be a punishment from God that ran in families. This belief led to moral judgments and ostracization of victims. Now known as Hansen's disease, it still afflicts tens of thousands of people a year and can be fatal if not treated with antibiotics.

1350: The Black Death

Responsible for the death of one-third of the world population, this second large outbreak of the Bubonic Plague possibly started in Asia and moved west in caravans. Entering through Sicily in 1347 A.D. when plague sufferers arrived in the port of Messina, it spread throughout Europe rapidly. Dead bodies became so prevalent that many remained rotting on the ground and created a constant stench in cities.

England and France were so incapacitated by the Plague that the countries called a truce to their war. The British feudal system collapsed when the Plague changed economic circumstances and demographics. Ravaging populations in Greenland, Vikings lost the strength to wage battle against native populations, and their exploration of North America halted.

1492: The Columbian Exchange

Following the arrival of the Spanish in the Caribbean, diseases such as smallpox, measles and Bubonic Plague were passed along to the native populations by the Europeans. With no previous exposure, these diseases devastated indigenous people, with as many as 90 percent dying throughout the north and south continents.

Upon arrival on the island of Hispaniola, Christopher Columbus encountered the Taino people, population 60,000. By 1548, the population stood at less than 500. This scenario repeated itself throughout the Americas.

In 1520, the Aztec Empire was destroyed by a smallpox infection. The disease killed many of its victims and incapacitated others. It weakened the population so much that they were unable to resist Spanish colonizers and left farmers unable to produce needed crops.

Research in 2019 even concluded that the deaths of some 56 million Native Americans in the 16th and 17th centuries, largely through disease, may have altered Earth's climate as vegetation growth on previously tilled land drew more CO2 from the atmosphere and caused a cooling event.

1665: The Great Plague of London

Following is a graph depicting the huge increase in deaths during the Great Plague of London in 1665 and 1666. The solid line shows all deaths and the broken line shows deaths attributed to the Plague.

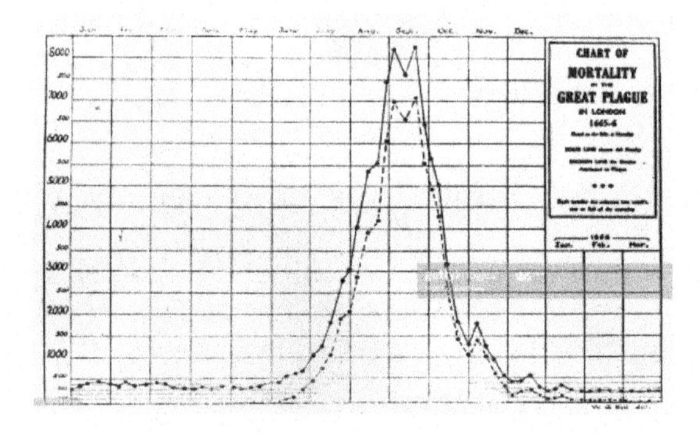

In another devastating appearance, the Bubonic Plague led to the deaths of 20 percent of London's population. As human death tolls mounted and mass graves appeared, hundreds of thousands of cats and dogs were slaughtered as the possible cause and the disease spread through ports along the Thames. The worst of the outbreak tapered off in the fall of 1666, around the same time as another destructive event occurred—the Great Fire of London.

1817: First Cholera Pandemic

The first of seven cholera pandemics over the next 150 years, this was a wave of the small intestinal infections originating in Russia, where one million people died. Spreading through feces-infected water and food, the bacterium was passed along to British soldiers who brought it to India where millions more died. The reach of the British Empire and its navy spread cholera to Spain, Africa, Indonesia, China, Japan, Italy, Germany, and America, where it killed 150,000 people. A vaccine was created in 1885, but the Pandemics continued.

1855: The Third Plague Pandemic

Starting in China and moving to India and Hong Kong, the Bubonic Plague claimed 15 million victims. Initially spread by fleas during a mining boom in Yunnan, the Plague is considered a factor in the Parthay rebellion and the Taiping rebellion.

India faced the most substantial casualties, and the Pandemic was used as an excuse for repressive policies that sparked some revolt against the British. The pandemic was considered active until 1960 when cases decreased to around two hundred.

1875: Fiji Measles Pandemic

After Fiji ceded to the British Empire, a royal party visited Australia as a gift from Queen Victoria. The royal party, who had arrived during a measles outbreak, brought the disease back to their island. It was spread further by the tribal heads and police who met with them upon their return.

Spreading quickly, the island was littered with corpses that were scavenged by wild animals. The populations of entire villages died and were burned down. Oftentimes, the sick were entrapped inside the fires. One-third of Fiji's population, a total of 40,000 people, died.

1889: Russian Flu

The first significant flu pandemic started in Siberia and Kazakhstan, traveled to Moscow, and made its way into Finland and then Poland, where it moved into the rest of Europe. By the following year, it had crossed the ocean into North America and Africa. By the end of 1890, 360,000 had died.

1918: Spanish Flu

The avian-borne flu resulted in 50 million deaths worldwide. The 1918 flu was first observed in Europe, the United States, and parts of Asia before swiftly spreading around the world. Wire service reports of a flu outbreak in Madrid in the Spring of 1918 led to the pandemic being called the "Spanish flu." At the time, there were no effective drugs or vaccines to treat this killer flu strain.

By October, hundreds of thousands of Americans died and body storage scarcity hit crisis level. But the flu threat disappeared in the summer of 1919 when most of the infected had either developed immunities or died. It is reported that October 1918 was the Deadliest Month ever in America.

1957: Asian flu

Starting in Hong Kong and spreading throughout China and then into the United States, the Asian flu became widespread in England where over six months, 14,000 people died. A second wave followed in early 1958, causing an estimated total of about 1.1 million deaths globally, with 116,000 deaths in the United States alone. A vaccine was developed, effectively containing the pandemic.

1981: HIV/AIDS

First identified in 1981, AIDS destroyed a person's immune system, resulting in eventual death by diseases that the body could usually fight off. Those infected by the HIV virus, encountered fever, headache, and enlarged lymph nodes. As symptoms subsided, carriers became highly infectious and were able to spread the disease through certain body and genital fluids. The disease also destroyed T-cells in the body.

AIDS was first observed in American homosexual communities but is believed to have been developed from a chimpanzee virus from West Africa in the 1920's. The disease moved to Haiti in the 1960's, and then New York and San Francisco in the 1970's.

Treatments have been developed to slow the progress of the disease, but 35 million people worldwide have died of AIDS since its discovery, and a cure is yet to be found.

2003: SARS

First identified in 2003 after several months of cases, Severe Acute Respiratory Syndrome (SARS) is believed to have possibly started with bats, spread to cats and then to humans in China, followed by 26 other countries; it is believed to have infected 8,096 people, causing 774 deaths.

SARS is characterized by respiratory problems, dry cough, fever and head and body aches and is spread through respiratory droplets from coughs and sneezes.

Quarantine efforts proved effective and by July of that year, the virus was contained and has not reappeared since. China was criticized for trying to suppress information about the virus at the beginning of the outbreak.

However, SARS was seen by global health professionals as a wake-up call to improve outbreak responses. Lessons from the pandemic were used to keep diseases like H1N1, Ebola and Zika under control.

2019: COVID-19

On March 11, 2020, the World Health Organization (WHO) announced that the COVID-19 virus was officially a pandemic after barreling through 114 countries in three months and infecting over

118,000 people. The spread is not anywhere near finished.

Covid-19 is caused by a novel new coronavirus strain that had not been previously contracted by people. Symptoms include respiratory problems, fever, and cough and can lead to pneumonia and death. Like SARS, it spreads through droplets from sneezes and coughs.

The first reported case in China appeared November 17, 2019, in the Hubei Province (Wuhan), but went unrecognized. Eight more cases appeared in December with researchers pointing to an unknown virus.

Many learned about COVID-19 when ophthalmologist Dr. Li Wenliang defied government orders and released safety information to other doctors. The following day, China informed the World Health Organization (WHO) and also charged Li with a crime.

Mysteriously, Li died from Covid-19 just over a month later.

Without a vaccine available, the virus spread beyond Chinese borders, and by mid-March, it had spread globally to more than 163 countries. On February 11, the infection was officially dubbed Covid-19.

The question has been asked whether there is significance to the astrological numerical occurrences of Pandemics. The Epilogue of this book will address this especially important question.

The Promise

Promises are always birthed out of pain. The promise of new life is encased in the labor pains of an expecting mother; but upon birth, there is delight and expectation of fulfillment of life. As believers, we must commit to envisioning a healthy and luminous future; one of continued growth and continued evolvement. We must bridle our faith and spiritual eyes to recognize that pain will only last so long. Scripture tells us that "weeping may endure for a night, but joy comes in the morning" (Psalm 30:5).

I recall the soft spoken, yet sincere words of my mother, "Nothing Ventured, Nothing Gained." Venturing is often not effortless and uncomplicated. As a matter of fact, when one goes on a venture, they understand that they are literally trekking into unchartered terrains. Often, they have elected to purposely challenge themselves to seek out the unknown despite the outcome.

I have noticed that in every instance, plagues served as a "wake-up" call or an awakening to a people, because there was a lack of obedience and trust or because of the presence of persistent sin. I ask the question, **Why Does It Take a Plague To Get Our Attention?**

There are many answers to this question, but I believe it can be best captured by the following statement: "We are placated beings whose goal is to avoid disruptions by any means possible". We love our comfort. However, we must recognize that our comfort zone can also be our danger zone. Never become too comfortable. Complacency tends to breed passivity, mediocrity and apathy. It tends to induce unacceptable levels of procrastination and encourages fearful inhibitions while triggering an innate desire to flee from the realities at hand.

- **NUGGET OF WISDOM: Nothing Bothers Us, Unless It Indeed Bothers Us.**

This often-touted thought process is unsustainable and equally untenable. It evokes a spirit of self-isolation and selfishness - twin beliefs that contradict the nature and Will of God. God entrusts us with an expectant mantle of righteousness. He wants us to give Him all the honor and reverence that is due Him. Oftentimes, we take His love and mercy for granted and diminish what He has done. Many churches and leaders have monetized the Word to bring self-wealth rather than to respect the place that God has positioned them. The fear of the Lord has been utterly abandoned and rationalized into oblivion by incalculable numbers of people.

God gives us seasons and time for repentance, but because we tend to be entangled in the tentacles of self-indulgence, self-actualization, and self-centeredness, we fail to heed the warnings. God, in His Divine love, always orchestrates an admonishment and the trumpets of warning before a plague. We have forgotten that He is the True

Vine and we are the branches. He resides within the very core of our spirits. Our very essence is intertwined in Him. “Let us make man in our image” is the existential foundation as human beings. As believers in Christ and His Word, our inextricable tethering to God is Life; It is Wisdom; It is Hope; It is Love; It is Understanding; It is the fruit of His Spirit and the gifting of His Mercy and Grace; He is our all and all. We unknowingly utter His reflection by the vibration of the sound “I am”. For He is the “Great I AM”. His stamp is literally upon us and our language reflects this reality. I am (God) grateful for His Love. I am (God) a willing and humble servant. I am (God) a member of His Body. Again, let me say, He is the Great I AM”. So be very cognizant and aware that whenever you utter the words “I Am”, you are evoking His unspeakable essence.

NUGGET OF WISDOM: When We Place Our Aspirations And Needs Ahead Of God, We Only Exist In "Provision" And Can Never Live In "Promise".

There are billions of people across this world, but they all have a common thread for self-perseverance. From biblical times until today, people have sought to satisfy their natural longings and desires. This is only a violation when it supersedes the mandate that "believers should love the Lord God with all of their mind, soul and

might."

This is a **"Key Reason**" that I believe God has allowed the Covid-19 Pandemic and other similar trials to impact our lives. The earth has been sifted through a perpetual sieve of signs and warnings. God is simply trying to get the world's attention and challenge its inhabitants to return to Him, because the Bridegroom is waiting. Judgment is real and we cannot ignore the facts. Over the past several decades, He has tried to awaken us with multiple destructive tsunamis, continuous wildfires and earthquakes, other natural disasters and world events i.e. – the World Trade Center Attack, the Sandy Hook Shooting, the Rwanda Genocide, the Boston Marathon Bombing, the Columbine Massacre, the Oklahoma City Bombing, the Norway Attacks in 2011, the Paris Terror Attacks in 2015, Hurricane Katrina, the Christ church Mosque Shootings and the Ebola Outbreak. This is a snapshot of recent history, with these scourges having occurred just in our lifetime, representing just two of the Horses of the Apocalypse (the Red horse, symbolizing war and bloodshed and the Pale horse identified as Death).

To add velocity to the winds of confusion, we are mired in corrupt politics, unnatural shifts in climate, divisive political unrest and overt and covert racial hatred evidenced by the senseless murders of people of color across this nation. In addition to constant social unrest, systemic racism, coupled with record low moralities, from the gravity of economic injustices to the anguish of race relations, it has consumed us as a people.

Unfortunately, as a defiant people, we became contrite for a fleeting moment, and then reverted to our usual tendencies of brazen contrariness and temerity. For many, a rather insolent, waffling, and vacillating form of godliness was displayed, but no sincere conviction was expressed relative to the clarion warnings from God. We failed to collectively establish within our hearts, mind, and actions a spiritual penance and attrition necessary to appease an "all knowing" and "all loving" Creator.

Injustices continue to persist, while believers sip from the goblet of misery, distress, and fatigue. We learned to concomitantly stream from our edifices of worship, with our usual self-pious dispositions but failed to honor and submissively engage with God in spirit and truth. We tend to be a rather cavalier and slothful in our approach to committing to pure worship ("worth-ship"); that's because true worship takes the total unselfish yielding of one's self, time and energy.

- **NUGGET OF WISDOM: Understand That "What Is A Surprise To Us Is A Not Surprise To God."**

The Coronavirus Pandemic of 2020 caused many to reflect and reassess their priorities. Our behaviors have been modified in a way that even those with iron-clad immune systems and ultra-positive mental constitutions dare to venture out and engage in their daily affairs without adorning a mask. Will it be like this forever? I do not believe so. But many things will indeed change. There will be Glory after this; and I believe that we will be stronger and wiser when all is said and done.

The one thing that this pandemic has not changed is **THE PROMISE**. God declared to Moses - "Therefore say unto the children of Israel, I am the

LORD, and I will bring you out from under the burdens of the Egyptians, and I will rescue you from their bondage, and I will redeem you with a stretched out arm, and with great judgments. And I will take you to me for a people, and I will be to you a God: and you shall know that I am the LORD your God, who brings you out from under the burdens of the Egyptians. And I will bring you into the land which I did swear to give it to Abraham, to Isaac, and to Jacob; and I will give it to you for a heritage: I am the LORD" (Exodus 6:6-8). We are heirs and joint heirs of the Promise.

The Promise is that He will be with us through the storms of life. The Promise is that if we walk through the valleys of death, He is with us. The Promise is one of deliverance and power. The Promise is one of blessings and wholeness. The Promise is that if we are faithful and obedient, we will partake of the fruit of the land. The Promise is of safety and salvation. The Promise is of good health and protection for you and your seed. The

Promise is of wealth and favor. The Promise is of Eternal Life.

Do not allow yourself to become weary or worn because of the present circumstances and apparent pressures. Do not allow a state of loneliness to overshadow you and emotionally shift you from a place of believing that God has all things under control. Before God does anything, He knows that He has already designed your expected end. He declared in His Word, "I know the thoughts that I have towards you, thoughts of good and not evil; to grant to you an expected end."

So yes, every avenue and thoroughfare of your life may seem rife with unbearable calamity; but I strongly encourage you to "find the good" in every circumstance – everything will be alright. Live out your lives with the expectation of something greater, while surrounding yourselves with individuals who share the same desire and passion for something greater. Scripture states in Philippians 4:8; "Whatsoever things are true, whatsoever things are honest, whatsoever things are just, whatsoever things are pure, whatsoever things are lovely, whatsoever things are of good report; if there be any virtue, and if there be any praise, think on these things."

You may ask, how does Valerie Daniels-Carter know? It is because I have learned to approach life from the methodology of "think on these things" as noted in Philippians Chapter 4. I encourage individuals daily to "accentuate the positive" and "diminish the negatives" (negative people, negative thoughts, and negative environments). Take time to learn how to be content.

Contentment is an act of acceptance. Paul teaches us that "whatever state I am in, to be content." Even when there are setbacks or distresses, you should calmly manage through them. Rage has never helped a bad situation; it only makes it worse. When you are filled with indignation, you only affect your well-being.

Adorn yourself with confidence; Seek to understand the solution and positively manage it. Have faith and know that God is in control. Faith equips you to operate within the place of destiny that God has for you. In Psalm 56:11, the psalmist writes, “In God I trust; I will not be afraid. What can man do to me?” What a breath-taking, awe-inspiring, and faith-filled declaration, which highlights the power of trusting in God. Regardless of what happens, the psalmist declares, “I will trust in God because I know He knows and understands what is best for me”.

Faith allows us to embrace this level of trust. Faith comes by hearing the Word of God; it comes through experiences with God and it comes by not allowing yourself to be consumed by deleterious and pessimistic people. Faith works in the affirmative. Faith and trust take courage.

- **NUGGET OF WISDOM: When You Are Content Knowing That God Is In Control, What Else Really Matters?**

Your faith must be secure for you to be content. It cannot be passive or wavering because: "A double-minded man is unstable in ALL of his ways." At some point, you must trust what you believe and exercise a tenacious commitment to live in that conviction. Everyone is struggling with how they will rebuild or reestablish themselves. Why burden yourself with this when it is not our job or responsibility? It is God's job, our Father's responsibility to make provision and position His children for blessings. We are charged with doing what we were created to do: to simply worship God.

We were created to reverence and adore Him. God does not need humanity's help to fulfill His Promises to you and me. He only requires our obedience and adherence to His Word. Chapter 6 of Hebrews teaches us that, "God is not unrighteous to forget your work and labor of love, which we have shewed toward His name, in that ye have ministered to the saints and do minister." Paul goes on to state that; "Surely blessing I will bless thee and multiplying I will multiply thee. And so, after he had patiently endured, he obtained the Promise." Is His Promise worth patiently waiting for? You better believe it is.

Take a moment and reflect on where you are. Conduct a candidly honest analysis and assessment of yourself. Remember no one knows you better than you. Whether you realize it or not, truth allows you to handle life challenges and circumstances better.

- **NUGGET OF WISDOM: To Deny Reality Is To Place The Inevitable On Hold; Allow Your Promise To Become A Reality.**

At this point you can wait and see what happens, hope nothing more happens or make something happen. You make it happen by allowing the Promise to become a reality in you. You make it happen by declaring I am the head, not the tail. You make it happen by sharing with others and seeking God for insight and direction. Never walk through a pandemic without understanding that your Purpose and Promise are determined by God, not man. Always have a spirit of thanksgiving and gratitude. As a matter of fact, take a moment right now and thank God for life, health, and wisdom. Thank Him for being a Promise-keeping God and for supplying all your needs. It is not hard to care for someone when you know their love is genuine. As I have stated on countless occasions, destiny is the place that God is taking those who have the courage to go. He is not going to force us to live in purpose. He opens the door of opportunity, but we must elect to opt-in. As students of Promise, we must learn to research the fundamental protocols that unfold blessings and ignite God to act on our behalf.

A few years ago, I had the opportunity to assist a Pastor in Africa. For the sake of this book, I will call his name "Pastor May I Have More Please." No matter what I did for this leader, at the end of our conversation his request was "May I Have More, Please." Being the philanthropist that I am, I would always try to accommodate his request because the need was so great. But there comes a time when the donor or giver needs to hear, "Thank You." Not that you seek glory or recognition, but simply an acknowledgement from the receiver that they are appreciative and grateful and that they understand the sacrifices that have been given for them to receive their gift.

Month after month, I would send donations, equipment, clothing, and food. Every month, I would receive an updated request of additional needs and wants, but never once did I ever receive a separate communication with a simple note of thanks. Initially, I did not allow it to bother me because my desire to be a blessing was greater than the ungraciousness of "Pastor May I Have More Please." One day, I received a request from a different pastor who not only requested assistance, but also acknowledged in his communications that "if you would be so kind to assist, we would forever be grateful." Immediately, without thought, it became my joy to give to the leader and his organization. It was not a struggle to share with someone who was thankful and appreciative. After receiving the donation, this leader emailed a card of appreciation from every child living in the orphanage, with no additional requests attached; Simply "thank you" and "we love you." "Thank you for our new shoes and clothes and oh by the way, that was the best meal we have ever eaten." As far as I am concerned, if I have capacity, those children will never go hungry.

I can only imagine how God feels when day after day He gives life, hope, and joy, and we fail to show admiration and love for what He has done. He gave His only Son so that we could have eternal life. His Son gave His life; what more could He do? Yet, we fail to simply say, "Thank You." If you want to live in His Promise and experience the wealth of His Greatness, I challenge you to be Grateful. Your gratefulness will unlock closed doors and take you to a level of receivership that only true believers can experience.

During this Covid-19 season or any transitional period, we should take time daily to be thankful. It is impossible to praise God and remain in a depressed state of mind at the same time. The minute you begin to shift your thoughts in a positive direction, negativity must dissipate. Darkness cannot abide where light is. Live in Promise and operate with integrity and watch God bring the increase.

During a training and empowerment session that I conducted in Michigan, I asked a division leader to walk everyone through what he believed was needed for the organization to achieve their objectives. He listed all the challenges as well as what he believed to be their deficiencies. In the middle of his presentation, I stopped him and stated, "If you are going to win, you must change your mindset, method of delivery, and raise your expectations." He glared at me and questioned me. He stated, "I am not being negative, these are just the facts." *I replied, "No one wants to work with negative people or individuals that cannot paint a clear roadmap to success". I told him, "You must accentuate the positive and strategically manage the areas of opportunity. Don't focus on what is wrong, look for what is good and begin building from there. Leaders challenge individuals to do their best and ignite hope in them."* If there is no hope or expectation of betterment to come, then a true winner will look for another opportunity. Innate within every propitious and confident individual is the desire to improve and to pursue purpose.

There is a battle going on in the spirit of all of us. Paul stated that “When we would do good, evil is ever present.” Negativity will always exist and those who elect to live under its control will never live in Purpose. The command to delight one’s self in God during the midst of devastation can be challenging and tough. But that is the only path to Promise. People cannot perform what is designed for God to implement. You must take your eyes off the circumstances and fix them on Christ and trust Him to do what is best, He is sovereign and He knows all things. God created us with the longing to admire the wonders of who He is and His excellent greatness.

- **NUGGET OF WISDOM: Knowing Your Purpose Will Allow You To Experience The Promise.**

When you delight in the Excellency of God, you will become keenly aware of the fact that He is the answer to your longings, deficiencies, and trouble.

Nobody and nothing can heal our soul diseases but God. When your soul is diseased, your vision is blurred and you cannot see Purpose. But when we devote ourselves to the Lord, He opens our understanding and brings good things to life as well as health and prosperity. Consider this quote from Puritan Preacher Jonathan Edward's sermon, *The Excellences of Christ*: "The person of Christ brings together infinite highness and infinite condescension, infinite justice and infinite grace, infinite glory and lowest humility, infinite majesty and transcendent meekness, deepest reverence towards God and equality with God, infinite worthiness of good and greatest patience under suffering evil, exceeding spirit of obedience with supreme dominion over heaven and earth, absolute sovereignty and perfect resignation, self-sufficiency and entire trust and reliance upon God."

When we seek God and trust Him for the greater as we delight ourselves in Him, it then becomes God's responsibility to provide Promise and Blessings. The only thing that disqualifies any believer from the Promises of God is when we pursue after things that are an abomination to Him. So, I encourage you to:

- Live a Life Pleasing to God
- Seek His Guidance and Walk By Faith
- Dismiss Negativity and Negative People
- Trust In The Lord With Your Total Being

My challenge to you is to make sure you are ready for the Promise. Consider the ant. Ants are one of the most industrious, socially successful organisms of God's creation. Ants hibernate in the winter. They look for warm places to spend the cold months and then become active again in the Spring. Seemingly, ants disappear as they strategically prepare for the changing of seasons. They are ready when it is time to shift. Ants never quit. When they are on the trail for food, they do not allow any obstacles to stand in their way. They leave a pheromone trail so that not only can they know where they've been, but it assists other ants trying to find their way on the trail behind them. They do not stand and wait for another ant to instruct them to get busy because "winter is coming". They are busy all summer preparing for their future. Proverb 30:25-28 declares: "The ants are a people not strong, yet they prepare their meat in the summer; The colonies are but a feeble folk, yet make they their houses in the rocks; The locusts have not king, yet go they forth all of them by bands, The spider taketh hold with her hands, and is in the kings palaces."

We must patiently prepare now for our time of blessings. If we wait until the changing of the season to seek Promise, we place ourselves at a significant disadvantage. I do believe during the end days there will be a great wealth transfer, but we must prepare now. God is preparing to send an abundance of divine blessings to His people, but we as a people must be ready. You can determine the height and depth of your blessing based on how well equipped you are. Behold the Bridegroom is coming, make sure your lamp is lit, and you have oil. Do not worry if others do not see what you see, it is because they are not going where you are going. Do not wait for man to validate you; God has already authenticated you. Know that you are connected to a greater Power and your Purpose is a "God Thing". Lastly, never wait for someone to lead you where God has Destined you to be, follow His path - - - - - -

And Watch God Take You From Pandemic To Promise

FROM PANDEMIC TO PROMISE

THE EPILOGUE

Now we shall return to the question: Is there significance to the astrological numerical occurrences of Pandemics?

The Bible definitely seems to use numbers in patterns or to teach a spiritual truth. The timing of an event is calendared to document and give evidence to its manifestation. Some people believe there is a scientific numeric timetable to the occurrences of pandemic events. I certainly am not a numerologist or knowledgeable enough to quantify such a definitive statement relative to the eschatological timing of Pandemics. However, I can declaratively state that a year is defined as "the orbital period of a planetary body, moving in its orbit around the Sun". A calendar year is an "approximation of the number of days of the

Earth's orbital period, as counted in a given calendar."

As a student of biblical study, I looked at each reflected year in which a pandemic occurred and wondered what behaviorism existed in the World at that time? I then contemplated on what did we learn from it, and how long did the reflective timeframe last before we reverted to a Nation that abandoned our God and placed our priorities ahead of Him.

I have concluded that whenever there are multiple reoccurrences of something, the timing and span of the incidence should be measured and recorded. In addition, the spiritual condition of the nation should considered and documented. In reflection, the reported Pandemics from 1855 to Covid-19 are some of the shortest time spans ever recorded. The levels of unrest and disregard for God worldwide during these periods were at an unprecedented high. The scripture in Mark 13:20-24states, "And except that the Lord had shortened those days, no flesh should be saved; but for the elects sake, whom he had chosen, he hath shortened the days. And then if any man shall say to you, Lo here is Christ; lo, he is there; believe him not: For false Christs and false prophets shall rise, and shall shew signs and wonders, to seduce, if it were possible, even the elect. But take ye heed: behold, I have foretold you all things."

Thus, we must ask ourselves; "When a nation forgets God, is it wrong for God to remove His hand of protection?" Rhetorically, it is easy for people to point the finger and say, "why would a loving God remove His protection and allow death and destruction"? But I look at the three fingers that are pointing back at me and instead of saying, "Why would God", I say, "Why would we?" Why would we be so selfish, disobedient, and self-centered? Why would we place worth ahead of worship? Why would we create division and strife? Why would we offer tainted sacrifices and last moment praise? Why would we allow the enemy to have dominion over our lives?

What is the answer to the question? Perhaps there is significance to the astrological numerical occurrences of pandemics. It is inevitable and expected that devastation and destruction will occur given the circumstance of this world. However, when we return to what His word teaches and develop a right relationship with God, He who is Forgiving, Faithful, and Almighty will restore to us Divine Blessings. He is indeed the God of all flesh and it is His good pleasure to give to us **THE PROMISE**.

It is just that simple.

SOURCE

1. Easton's Bible Dictionary
2. Free Dictionary by Farlex
3. The King James Version of the Bible
4. Disease and History by Frederick C. Cartwright, published by Sutton Publishing, 2014.

   Disease: The Story of Disease and Mankind's Continuing Struggle Against It by Mary Dobson, published by Quercus, 2007. Encyclopedia of Pestilence, Pandemics, and Plagues by Ed, Joseph P. Byrne, published by Greenwood Press, 2008. Influenza, The American Experience.

   Source Book of Medical History, Logan Clendening, published by Dover Publications, 1960. Citation Information Article Title Pandemics That Changed History Author History.com Editors Website Name HISTORY

   URL https://www.history.com/topics/middle-ages/Pandemics-timeline Updated May 19, 2020 Original Published Date February 27, 2019 TAGSPANDEMICS BY HISTORY.COM EDITORS
5. Puritan Preacher Jonathan Edward's sermon "The Excellences of Christ".

6. Editing and Review: Daren Daniels, Dr. Paula Ellis and Lisa Townsel
7. Printed By: Eagle Flair Graphics and Printing (Milwaukee, WI)
8. Special acknowledgements to Bishop Sedgwick Daniels and Dr. Lisa Winters-Smith.

FROM PANDEMIC TO PROMISE

Made in USA - Kendallville, IN
1187644_9781636493152
10.30.2020 0824